Biographical Sketches

Nathaniel Hawthorne

Contents

MRS. HUTCHINSON.	7
SIR WILLIAM PHIPS	14
SIR WILLIAM PEPPERELL.	19
THOMAS GREEN FESSENDEN.	26
JONATHAN CILLEY.	38

BIOGRAPHICAL SKETCHES

BY

Nathaniel Hawthorne

MRS. HUTCHINSON.

The character of this female suggests a train of thought which will form as natural an Introduction to her story, as most of the Prefaces to Gay's Fables, or the tales of Prior; besides that, the general soundness of the moral may excuse any want of present applicability. We will not look for a living resemblance of Mrs. Hutchinson, though the search might not be altogether fruitless. But there are portentous indications, changes gradually taking place in the habits and feelings of the gentle sex, which seem to threaten our posterity with many of those public women, whereof one was a burden too grievous for our fathers. The press, however, is now the medium through which feminine ambition chiefly manifests itself; and we will not anticipate the period (trusting to be gone hence ere it arrive) when fair orators shall be as numerous as the fair authors of our own day. The hastiest glance may show how much of the texture and body of cis-atlantic literature is the work of those slender fingers from which only a light and fanciful embroidery has heretofore been required, that might sparkle upon the garment without enfeebling the web. Woman's intellect should never give the tone to that of man; and even her morality is not exactly the material for masculine virtue. A false liberality, which mistakes the strong division-lines of Nature for arbitrary distinctions, and a courtesy, which might polish criticism, but should never soften it, have done their best to add a girlish feebleness to the tottering infancy of our literature. The evil is likely to be a growing one. As yet, the great body of American women are a domestic race; but when a continuance of ill-judged incitements shall have turned their hearts away from the fireside, there are obvious circumstances which will render female pens more numerous and more prolific than those of men, though but equally encouraged; and (limited, of course, by the scanty support of the public, but increasing indefinitely within those limits) the ink-stained Amazons will expel their rivals by actual pressure, and petticoats wave triumphantly over all the field. But, allowing that such forebodings are slightly exaggerated, is it good for woman's self that the path of feverish hope, of tremulous success, of bitter and ignominious disappointment, should be left wide open to her? Is the prize worth her having, if she win it? Fame does not increase the peculiar respect which men pay to female excellence, and there is a delicacy (even in rude bosoms, where few would think to find it) that perceives, or fancies, a sort of impropriety in the display of woman's natal mind to the gaze of the world, with indications by which its inmost secrets may be searched out. In fine, criticism should examine with a stricter, instead of a more indulgent eye, the merits of females at its bar, because they are to justify themselves for an irregularity which men do not commit in appearing there; and woman, when she feels the impulse of genius like a command of Heaven within her, should be aware that she is relinquishing a part of the loveliness of her sex, and obey the inward voice with sorrowing reluctance, like the Arabian maid who bewailed the gift of prophecy. Hinting thus imperfectly at sentiments which may be developed on a future occasion, we proceed to consider the celebrated subject of this sketch.

Mrs. Hutchinson was a woman of extraordinary talent and strong imagination, whom the latter quality, following the general direction taken by the enthusiasm of the times, prompted to stand forth as a reformer in religion. In her native country, she had shown symptoms of irregular and daring thought, but, chiefly by the influence of a favorite pastor, was restrained from open indiscretion. On the removal of this clergyman, becoming dissatisfied with the ministry under which she lived, she was drawn in by the great tide of Puritan emigration, and visited Massachusetts within a few years after its first settlement. But she bore trouble in her own bosom, and could find no peace in this chosen land. She soon began to promulgate strange and dangerous opinions, tending, in the peculiar situation of the colony, and from the principles which were its basis, and indispensable for its temporary support, to eat into its very existence. We shall endeavor to give a more practical idea of this part of her course.

It is a summer evening. The dusk has settled heavily upon the woods, the waves, and the Trimountain peninsula, increasing that dismal aspect of the embryo town, which was said to have drawn tears of despondency from Mrs. Hutchinson, though she believed that her mission thither was divine. The houses, straw thatched and lowly roofed, stand irregularly along streets that are yet roughened by the roots of the trees, as if the forest, departing at the approach of man, had left its reluctant footprints behind. Most of the dwellings are lonely and silent: from a few we may hear the reading of some sacred text, or the quiet voice of prayer; but nearly all the sombre life of the scene is collected near the extremity of the village. A crowd of hooded women, and of men in steeple-hats and close-cropped hair, are assembled at the door and open windows of a house newly built. An earnest expression glows in every face; and some press inward, as if the bread of life were to be dealt forth, and they feared to lose their share; while others would fain hold them back, but enter with them, since they may not be restrained. We, also, will go in, edging through the thronged doorway to an apartment which occupies the whole breadth of the house. At the upper end, behind a table, on which are placed the Scriptures and two glimmering lamps, we see a woman, plainly attired, as befits her ripened years: her hair, complexion, and eyes are dark, the latter somewhat dull and heavy, but kindling up with a gradual brightness. Let us look round upon the hearers. At her right hand his countenance suiting well with the gloomy light which discovers it, stands Vane, the youthful governor, preferred by a hasty judgment of the people over all the wise and hoary heads that had preceded him to New England. In his mysterious eyes we may read a dark enthusiasm, akin to that of the woman whose cause he has espoused, combined with a shrewd worldly foresight, which tells him that her doctrines will be productive of change and tumult, the elements of his power and delight. On her left, yet slightly drawn back, so as to evince a less decided support, is Cotton, no young and hot enthusiast, but a mild, grave man in the decline of life, deep in all the learning of the age, and sanctified in heart, and made venerable in feature, by the long exercise of his holy profession. He, also, is deceived by the strange fire now laid upon the altar; and he alone among his brethren is excepted in the denunciation of the new apostle, as sealed and set apart by Heaven to the work of the ministry. Others of the priesthood stand full in front of the woman, striving to beat her down with brows of wrinkled iron, and whispering sternly and significantly among themselves as she unfolds her seditious doctrines, and grows warm in their support. Foremost is Hugh Peters, full of holy wrath, and scarce containing himself from rushing forward to convict her of damnable heresies. There, also, is Ward, meditating a reply of empty puns, and quaint antitheses, and tinkling jests that puzzle us with nothing but a sound. The audience are variously affected; but none are indifferent. On the foreheads of the aged, the mature, and strong-minded, you may generally read steadfast disapprobation, though here and there is one whose faith seems shaken in those whom lie had trusted for years. The females, on the other hand, are shuddering and weeping, and at times they cast a desolate look of fear around them; while the young men lean forward, fiery and impatient, fit instruments for whatever rash deed may be suggested. And what is the eloquence that gives rise to all these passions? The woman tells then (and cites texts from the Holy Book to prove her words) that they have put their trust in unregenerated and uncommissioned men, and have followed them into the wilderness for nought. Therefore their hearts are turning from those whom they had chosen to lead them to heaven; and they feel like children who have been enticed far from home, and see the features of their guides change all at once, assuming a fiendish shape in some frightful solitude.

These proceedings of Mrs. Hutchinson could not long be endured by the provincial government. The present was a most remarkable case, in which religious freedom was wholly inconsistent with public safety, and where the principles of an illiberal age indicated the very course which must have been pursued by worldly policy and enlightened wisdom. Unity of faith was the star that had guided these people over the deep; and a diversity of sects would either have scattered them from the land to which they had as yet so few attachments, or, perhaps, have excited a diminutive civil war among those who had come so far to worship together. The opposition to what may be termed the Established Church had now lost its chief support by the removal of Vane from office, and his departure for England; and Mr. Cotton began to have that light in regard to his errors, which will sometimes break in upon the wisest and most pious men, when their opinions are unhappily discordant with those of the powers that be. A synod, the first in New England, was speedily assembled, and pronounced its condemnation of the obnoxious doctrines. Mrs. Hutchinson was next summoned before the supreme civil tribunal, at which, however, the most eminent of the clergy were present, and appear to have taken a very active part as witnesses and advisers. We shall here resume the more picturesque style of narration.

It is a place of humble aspect where the elders of the people are met, sitting in judgment upon the disturber of Israel. The floor of the low and narrow hall is laid with planks hewn by the axe; the beams of the roof still wear the rugged bark with which they grew up in the forest; and the hearth is formed of one broad, un-hammered stone, heaped with logs that roll their blaze and smoke up a chimney of wood and clay. A sleety shower beats fitfully against the windows, driven by the November blast, which comes howling onward from the northern desert, the boisterous and unwelcome herald of a New England winter. Rude benches are arranged across the apartment, and along its sides, occupied by men whose piety and learning might have entitled them to seats in those high councils of the ancient church, whence opinions were sent forth to confirm or supersede the gospel in the belief of the whole world and of posterity. Here are collected all those blessed fathers of the land, who rank in our veneration next to the evangelists of Holy Writ; and here, also, are many, unpurified from the fiercest errors of the age, and ready to propagate the religion of peace by violence. In the highest place sits Winthrop,--a man by whom the innocent and guilty might alike desire to be judged; the first confiding in his integrity and wisdom, the latter hoping in his mildness, Next is Endicott, who would stand with his drawn sword at the gate of heaven, and resist to the death all pilgrims thither, except they travelled his own path. The infant eyes of one in this assembly beheld the fagots blazing round the martyrs in Bloody Mary's time: in later life he dwelt long at Leyden, with the first who went from England for conscience' sake; and now, in his weary age, it matters little where he lies down to die. There are others whose hearts were smitten in the high meridian of ambitious hope, and whose dreams still tempt them with the pomp of the Old World and the din of its crowded cities, gleaming and echoing over the deep. In the midst, and in the centre of all eyes, we see the woman. She stands loftily before her judges with a determined brow; and, unknown to herself, there is a flash of carnal pride half hidden in her eye, as she surveys the many learned and famous men whom her doctrines have put in fear. They question her; and her answers are ready and acute: she reasons with them shrewdly, and brings Scripture in support of every argument. The deepest controversialists of that scholastic day find here a woman, whom all their trained and sharpened intellects are inadequate to foil. But, by the excitement of the contest, her heart is made to rise and swell within her, and she bursts forth into eloquence. She tells them of the long unquietness which she had endured in England, perceiving the corruption of the Church, and yearning for a purer and more perfect light, and how, in a day of solitary prayer, that light was given. She claims for herself the peculiar power of distinguishing between the chosen of man, and the sealed of Heaven, and affirms that her gifted eye can see the glory round the foreheads of saints, sojourning in their mortal state. She declares herself commissioned to separate the true shepherds from the false, and denounces present and future judgments on the laud, if she be disturbed in her celestial errand. Thus the accusations are proved from her own mouth. Her judges hesitate; and some speak faintly in her defence; but, with a few dissenting voices, sentence is pronounced, bidding her go out from among them, and trouble the land no more.

Mrs. Hutchinson's adherents throughout the colony were now disarmed; and she proceeded to Rhode Island, an accustomed refuge for the exiles of Massachusetts in all seasons of persecution. Her enemies believed that the anger of Heaven was following her, of which Governor Winthrop does not disdain to record a notable instance, very interesting in a scientific point of view, but fitter for his old and homely narrative than for modern repetition. In a little time, also, she lost her husband, who is mentioned in history only as attending her footsteps, and whom we may conclude to have been (like most husbands of celebrated women) a mere insignificant appendage of his mightier wife. She now grew uneasy away frown the Rhode Island colonists, whose liberality towards her, at an era when liberality was not esteemed a Christian virtue, probably arose from a comparative insolicitude on religious matters, more distasteful to Mrs. Hutchinson than even the uncompromising narrowness of the Puritans. Her final movement was to lead her family within the limits of the Dutch jurisdiction, where, having felled the trees of a virgin soil, she became herself the virtual head, civil and ecclesiastical, of a little colony.

Perhaps here she found the repose hitherto so vainly sought. Secluded from all whose faith she could not govern, surrounded by the dependants over whom she held an unlimited influence, agitated by none of the tumultuous billows which were left swelling behind her, we may suppose that, in the stillness of Nature, her heart was stilled. But her impressive story was to have an awful close. Her last scene is as difficult to be described as a shipwreck, where the shrieks of the victims die unheard, along a desolate sea, and a shapeless mass of agony is all that can be brought home to the imagination. The savage foe was on the watch for blood. Sixteen persons assembled at the evening prayer: in the deep midnight their cry rang through the forest; and daylight dawned upon the lifeless clay of all but one. It was a circumstance not to be unnoticed by our stern ancestors, in considering the fate of her who had so troubled their religion, that an infant daughter, the sole survivor amid the terrible destruction of her mother's household, was bred in a barbarous faith, and never learned the way to the Christian's heaven. Yet we will hope that there the mother and child have met.

SIR WILLIAM PHIPS.

Few of the personages of past times (except such as have gained renown in fireside legends as well as in written history) are anything more than mere names to their successors. They seldom stand up in our imaginations like men. The knowledge communicated by the historian and biographer is analogous to that which we acquire of a country by the map,--minute, perhaps, and accurate, and available for all necessary purposes, but cold and naked, and wholly destitute of the mimic charm produced by landscape-painting. These defects are partly remediable, and even without an absolute violation of literal truth, although by methods rightfully interdicted to professors of biographical exactness. A license must be assumed in brightening the materials which time has rusted, and in tracing out half-obliterated inscriptions on the columns of antiquity: Fancy must throw her reviving light on the faded incidents that indicate character, whence a ray will be reflected, more or less vividly, on the person to be described. The portrait of the ancient governor whose name stands at the head of this article will owe any interest it may possess, not to his internal self, but to certain peculiarities of his fortune. These must be briefly noticed.

The birth and early life of Sir William Phips were rather an extraordinary prelude to his subsequent distinction. He was one of the twenty-six children of a gunsmith, who exercised his trade--where hunting and war must have given it a full encouragement--in a small frontier settlement near the mouth of the river Kennebec. Within the boundaries of the Puritan provinces, and wherever those governments extended an effectual sway, no depth nor solitude of the wilderness could exclude youth from all the common opportunities of moral, and far more than common ones of religious education. Each settlement of the Pilgrims was a little piece of the Old World inserted into the New. It was like Gideon's fleece, unwet with dew: the desert wind that breathed over it left none of its wild influences there. But the first settlers of Maine and New Hampshire were led thither entirely by carnal motives: their governments were feeble, uncertain, sometimes nominally annexed to their sister colonies, and sometimes asserting a troubled independence. Their rulers might be deemed, in more than one instance, lawless adventurers, who found that security in the forest which they had forfeited in Europe. Their clergy (unlike that revered band who acquired so singular a fame elsewhere in New England) were too often destitute of the religious fervor which should have kept them in the track of virtue, unaided by the restraints of human law and the dread of worldly dishonor; and there are records of lamentable lapses on the part of those holy men, which, if we may argue the disorder of the sheep from the unfitness of the shepherd, tell a sad tale as to the morality of the eastern provinces. In this state of society, the future governor grew up; and many years after, sailing with a fleet and an army to make war upon the French, he pointed out the very hills where he had reached the age of manhood, unskilled even to read and write. The contrast between the commencement and close of his life was the effect of casual circumstances. During a considerable time, he was a mariner, at a period when there was much license on the high-seas. After attaining to some rank in the English navy, he heard of an ancient Spanish wreck off the coast of Hispaniola, of such mighty value, that, according to the stories of the day, the sunken gold might be seen to glisten, and the diamonds to flash, as the triumphant billows tossed about their spoil. These treasures of the deep (by the aid of certain noblemen, who claimed the lion's share) Sir William Phips sought for, and recovered, and was sufficiently enriched, even after an honest settlement with the partners of his adventure. That the land might give him honor, as the sea had given him wealth, he received knighthood from King James. Returning to New England, he professed repentance of his sins (of which, from the nature both of his early and more recent life, there could scarce fail to be some slight accumulation), was baptized, and, on the accession of the Prince of Orange to the throne, became the first governor under the second charter. And now, having arranged these preliminaries, we shall attempt to picture forth a day of Sir William's life, introducing no very remarkable events, because history supplies us with none such convertible to our purpose.

    It is the forenoon of a day in summer, shortly after the governor's arrival; and he stands upon his doorsteps, preparatory to a walk through the metropolis. Sir William is a stout man, an inch or two below the middle size, and rather beyond the middle point of life. His dress is of velvet,--a dark purple, broadly embroidered; and his sword-hilt and the lion's head of his cane display specimens of the gold from the Spanish wreck. On his head, in the fashion of the court of Louis XIV., is a superb full-bottomed periwig, amid whose heap of ringlets his face shows like a rough pebble in the setting that befits a diamond. Just emerging from the door are two footmen,--one an African slave of shining ebony, the other an English bondservant, the property of the governor for a term of years. As Sir William comes down the steps, he is met by three elderly gentlemen in black, grave and solemn as three tombstones on a ramble from the burying-ground. These are ministers of the town, among whom we recognize Dr. Increase Mather, the late provincial agent at the English court, the author of the present governor's appointment, and the right arm of his administration. Here follow many bows and a deal of angular politeness on both sides. Sir William professes his anxiety to re-enter the house, and give audience to the reverend gentlemen: they, on the other hand, cannot think of interrupting his walk; and the courteous dispute is concluded by a junction of the parties; Sir William and Dr. Mather setting forth side by side, the two other clergymen forming the centre of the column, and the black and white footmen bringing up the rear. The business in hand relates to the dealings of Satan in the town of Salem. Upon this subject, the principal ministers of the province have been consulted; and these three eminent persons are their deputies, commissioned to express a doubtful opinion, implying, upon the whole, an exhortation to speedy and vigorous measures against the accused. To such councils, Sir William, bred in the forest and on the ocean, and tinctured with the superstition of both, is well inclined to listen.

As the dignitaries of Church and State make their way beneath the overhanging houses, the lattices are thrust ajar, and you may discern, just in the boundaries of light and shade, the prim faces of the little Puritan damsels, eying the magnificent governor, and envious of the bolder curiosity of the men. Another object of almost equal interest now appears in the middle of the way. It is a man clad in a hunting-shirt and Indian stockings, and armed with a long gun. His feet have been wet with the waters of many an inland lake and stream; and the leaves and twigs of the tangled wilderness are intertwined with his garments: on his head he wears a trophy which we would not venture to record without good evidence of the fact,--a wig made of the long and straight black hair of his slain savage enemies. This grim old heathen stands bewildered in the midst of King Street. The governor regards him attentively, and, recognizing a playmate of his youth, accosts him with a gracious smile, inquires as to the prosperity of their birthplace, and the life or death of their ancient neighbors, and makes appropriate remarks on the different stations allotted by fortune to two individuals born and bred beside the same wild river. Finally he puts into his hand, at parting, a shilling of the Massachusetts coinage, stamped with the figure of a stubbed pine-tree, mistaken by King Charles for the oak which saved his royal life. Then all the people praise the humility and bountifulness of the good governor, who struts onward flourishing his gold-headed cane; while the gentleman in the straight black wig is left with a pretty accurate idea of the distance between himself and his old companion. Meantime, Sir William steers his course towards the town dock. A gallant figure is seen approaching on the opposite side of the street, in a naval uniform profusely laced, and with a cutlass swinging by his side. This is Captain Short, the commander of a frigate in the service of the English king, now lying in the harbor. Sir William bristles up at sight of him, and crosses the street with a lowering front, unmindful of the hints of Dr. Mather, who is aware of an unsettled dispute between the captain and the governor, relative to the authority of the latter over a king's ship on the provincial station. Into this thorny subject, Sir William plunges headlong. The captain makes answer with less deference than the dignity of the potentate requires: the affair grows hot; and the clergymen endeavor to interfere in the blessed capacity of peacemakers. The governor lifts his cane; and the captain lays his hand upon his sword, but is prevented from drawing by the zealous exertions of Dr. Mather. There is a furious stamping of feet, and a mighty uproar from every mouth, in the midst of which his Excellency inflicts several very sufficient whacks on the head of the unhappy Short. Having thus avenged himself by manual force, as befits a woodman and a mariner, he vindicates the insulted majesty of the governor by committing his antagonist to prison. This done, Sir William removes his periwig, wipes away the sweat of the encounter, and gradually composes himself, giving vent, to a few oaths, like the subsiding ebullitions of a pot that has boiled over.

It being now near twelve o'clock, the three ministers are bidden to dinner at the governor's table, where the party is completed by a few Old Charter senators,--men reared at the feet of the Pilgrims, and who remember the days when Cromwell was a nursing-father to New England. Sir William presides with commendable decorum till grace is said, and the cloth removed. Then, as the grape-juice glides warm into the ventricles of his heart, it produces a change, like that of a running stream upon enchanted shapes; and the rude man of the sea and wilderness appears in the very chair where the stately governor sat down. He overflows with jovial tales of the forecastle and of his father's hut, and stares to see the gravity of his guests become more and more portentous in exact proportion as his own merriment increases. A noise of drum and fife fortunately breaks up the session.

The governor and his guests go forth, like men bound upon some grave business, to inspect the trainbands of the town. A great crowd of people is collected on the common, composed of whole families, from the hoary grandsire to the child of three years. All ages and both sexes look with interest on the array of their defenders; and here and there stand a few dark Indians in their blankets, dull spectators of the strength that has swept away their race. The soldiers wear a proud and martial mien, conscious that beauty will reward them with her approving glances; not to mention that there are a few less influential motives to contribute to keep up an heroic spirit, such as the dread of being made to "ride the wooden horse" (a very disagreeable mode of equestrian exercise,--hard riding, in the strictest sense), or of being "laid neck and heels," in a position of more compendiousness than comfort. Sir William perceives some error in their tactics, and places himself with drawn sword at their head. After a variety of weary evolutions, evening begins to fall, like the veil of gray and misty years that have rolled betwixt that warlike band and us. They are drawn into a hollow square, the officers in the centre; and the governor (for John Dunton's authority will bear us out in this particular) leans his hands upon his sword-hilt, and closes the exercises of the day with a prayer.

SIR WILLIAM PEPPERELL.

The mighty man of Kittery has a double claim to remembrance. He was a famous general, the most prominent military character in our ante- Revolutionary annals; and he may be taken as the representative of a class of warriors peculiar to their age and country,--true citizen- soldiers, who diversified a life of commerce or agriculture by the episode of a city sacked, or a battle won, and, having stamped their names on the page of history, went back to the routine of peaceful occupation. Sir William Pepperell's letters, written at the most critical period of his career, and his conduct then and at other times, indicate a man of plain good sense, with a large share of quiet resolution, and but little of an enterprising spirit, unless aroused by external circumstances. The Methodistic principles, with which he was slightly tinctured, instead of impelling him to extravagance, assimilated themselves to his orderly habits of thought and action. Thus respectably endowed, we find him, when near the age of fifty, a merchant of weight in foreign and domestic trade, a provincial counsellor, and colonel of the York County militia, filling a large space in the eyes of his generation, but likely to gain no other posthumous memorial than the letters on his tombstone, because undistinguished from the many worshipful gentlemen who had lived prosperously and died peacefully before him. But in the year 1745, an expedition was projected against Louisburg, a walled city of the French in the island of Cape Breton. The idea of reducing this strong fortress was conceived by William Vaughan, a bold, energetic, and imaginative adventurer, and adopted by Governor Shirley, the most bustling, though not the wisest ruler, that ever presided over Massachusetts. His influence at its utmost stretch carried the measure by a majority of only one vote in the legislature: the other New England provinces consented to lend their assistance; and the next point was to select a commander from among the gentlemen of the country, none of whom had the least particle of scientific soldiership, although some were experienced in the irregular warfare of the frontiers. In the absence of the usual qualifications for military rank, the choice was guided by other motives, and fell upon Colonel Pepperell, who, as a landed proprietor in three provinces, and popular with all classes of people, might draw the greatest number of recruits to his banner. When this doubtful speculation was proposed to the prudent merchant, he sought advice from the celebrated Whitefield, then an itinerant preacher in the country, and an object of vast antipathy to many of the settled ministers. The response of the apostle of Methodism, though dark as those of the Oracle of Delphos, intimating that the blood of the slain would be laid to Colonel Pepperell's charge, in case of failure, and that the envy of the living would persecute him, if victorious, decided him to gird on his armor. That the French might be taken unawares, the legislature had been laid under an oath of secrecy while their deliberations should continue; this precaution, however, was nullified by the pious perjury of a country member of the lower house, who, in the performance of domestic worship at his lodgings, broke into a fervent and involuntary petition for the success of the enterprise against Louisburg. We of the present generation, whose hearts have never been heated and amalgamated by one universal passion, and who are, perhaps, less excitable in the mass than our fathers, cannot easily conceive the enthusiasm with which the people seized upon the project. A desire to prove in the eyes of England the courage of her provinces; the real necessity for the destruction of this Dunkirk of America; the hope of private advantage; a remnant of the old Puritan detestation of Papist idolatry; a strong hereditary hatred of the French, who, for half a hundred years, had shed the blood of the English settlers in concert with the savages; the natural proneness of the New-Englanders to engage in temporary undertakings, even though doubtful and hazardous, such were some of the motives which soon drew together a host, comprehending nearly all the effective force of the country. The officers were grave deacons, justices of the peace, and other similar dignitaries; and in the ranks were many warm householders, sons of rich farmers, mechanics in thriving business, husbands weary of their wives, and bachelors disconsolate for want of them. The disciples of Whitefield also turned their excited imaginations in this direction, and increased the resemblance borne by the provincial army to the motley assemblages of the first crusaders. A part of the peculiarities of the affair may be grouped in one picture, by selecting the moment of General Pepperell's embarkation.

It is a bright and breezy day of March; and about twenty small white clouds are scudding seaward before the wind, airy forerunners of the fleet of privateers and transports that spread their sails to the sunshine in the harbor. The tide is at its height; and the gunwale of a barge alternately rises above the wharf, and then sinks from view, as it lies rocking on the waves in readiness to convey the general and his suite on board the Shirley galley. In the background, the dark wooden dwellings of the town have poured forth their inhabitants; and this way rolls an earnest throng, with the great man of the day walking in the midst. Before him struts a guard of honor, selected from the yeomanry of his own neighborhood, and stout young rustics in their Sunday clothes; next appear six figures who demand our more minute attention. He in the centre is the general, a well-proportioned man with a slight hoar-frost of age just visible upon him; he views the fleet in which lie is about to embark, with no stronger expression than a calm anxiety, as if he were sending a freight of his own merchandise to Europe. A scarlet British uniform, made of the best of broadcloth, because imported by himself, adorns his person; and in the left pocket of a large buff waistcoat, near the pommel of his sword, we see the square protuberance of a small Bible, which certainly may benefit his pious soul, and, perchance, may keep a bullet from his body. The middle-aged gentleman at his right hand, to whom he pays such grave attention, in silk, gold, and velvet, and with a pair of spectacles thrust above his forehead, is Governor Shirley. The quick motion of his small eyes in their puckered sockets, his grasp on one of the general's bright military buttons, the gesticulation of his forefinger, keeping time with the earnest rapidity of his words, have all something characteristic. His mind is calculated to fill up the wild conceptions of other men with its own minute ingenuities; and he seeks, as it were, to climb up to the moon by piling pebble-stones, one upon another. He is now impressing on the general's recollection the voluminous details of a plan for surprising Louisburg in the depth of midnight, and thus to finish the campaign within twelve hours after the arrival of the troops. On the left, forming a striking contrast with the unruffled deportment of Pepperell, and the fidgety vehemence of Shirley, is the martial figure of Vaughan: with one hand he has seized the general's arm; and he points the other to the sails of the vessel fluttering in the breeze, while the fire of his inward enthusiasm glows through his dark complexion, and flashes in tips of flame from his eyes. Another pale and emaciated person, in neglected and scarcely decent attire, and distinguished by the abstracted fervor of his manner, presses through the crowd, and attempts to lay hold of Pepperell's skirt. He has spent years in wild and shadowy studies, and has searched the crucible of the alchemist for gold, and wasted the life allotted him, in a weary effort to render it immortal. The din of warlike preparation has broken in upon his solitude; and he comes forth with a fancy of his half-maddened brain,-- the model of a flying bridge,--by which the army is to be transported into the heart of the hostile fortress with the celerity of magic. But who is this, of the mild and venerable countenance shaded by locks of a hallowed whiteness, looking like Peace with its gentle thoughts in the midst of uproar and stern designs? It is the minister of an inland parish, who, after much prayer and fasting, advised by the elders of the church and the wife of his bosom, has taken his staff, and journeyed townward. The benevolent old man would fair solicit the general's attention to a method of avoiding danger from the explosion of mines, and of overcoming the city without bloodshed of friend or enemy. We start as we turn from this picture of Christian love to the dark enthusiast close beside him,--a preacher of the new sect, in every wrinkled line of whose visage we can read the stormy passions that have chosen religion for their outlet. Woe to the wretch that shall seek mercy there! At his back is slung an axe, wherewith he goes to hew down the carved altars and idolatrous images in the Popish churches; and over his head he rears a banner, which, as the wind unfolds it, displays the motto given by Whitefield,--Christo Duce,--in letters red as blood. But the tide is now ebbing; and the general makes his adieus to the governor, and enters the boat: it bounds swiftly over the waves, the holy banner fluttering in the bows: a huzza from the fleet comes riotously to the shore; and the people thunder back their many-voiced reply.

When the expedition sailed, the projectors could not reasonably rely on assistance from the mother-country. At Canso, however, the fleet was strengthened by a squadron of British ships-of-the-lice and frigates, under Commodore Warren; and this circumstance undoubtedly prevented a discomfiture, although the active business, and all the dangers of the siege, fell to the share of the provincials. If we had any confidence that it could be done with half so much pleasure to the reader as to ourself, we would present, a whole gallery of pictures from these rich and fresh historic scenes. Never, certainly, since man first indulged his instinctive appetite for war, did a queerer and less manageable host sit down before a hostile city. The officers, drawn from the same class of citizens with the rank and file, had neither the power to institute an awful discipline, nor enough of the trained soldier's spirit to attempt it. Of headlong valor, when occasion offered, there was no lack, nor of a readiness to encounter severe fatigue; but, with few intermissions, the provincial army made the siege one long day of frolic and disorder. Conscious that no military virtues of their own deserved the prosperous result which followed, they insisted that Heaven had fought as manifestly on their side as ever on that of Israel in the battles of the Old Testament. We, however, if we consider the events of after-years, and confine our view to a period short of the Revolution, might doubt whether the victory was granted to our fathers as a blessing or as a judgment. Most of the young men who had left their paternal firesides, sound in constitution, and pure in morals, if they returned at all, returned with ruined health, and with minds so broken up by the interval of riot, that they never after could resume the habits of good citizenship. A lust for military glory was also awakened in the country; and France and England gratified it with enough of slaughter; the former seeking to recover what she had lost, the latter to complete the conquest which the colonists had begun. There was a brief season of repose, and then a fiercer contest, raging almost from end to end of North America. Some went forth, and met the red men of the wilderness; and when years had rolled, and the settler came in peace where they had come in war, there he found their unburied bones among the fallen boughs and withered leaves of many autumns. Others were foremost in the battles of the Canadas, till, in the day that saw the downfall of the French dominion, they poured their blood with Wolfe on the Heights of Abraham. Through all this troubled time, the flower of the youth were cut down by the sword, or died of physical diseases, or became unprofitable citizens by moral ones contracted in the camp and field. Dr. Douglass, a shrewd Scotch physician of the last century, who died before war had gathered in half its harvest, computes that many thousand blooming damsels, capable and well inclined to serve the state as wives and mothers, were compelled to lead lives of barren celibacy by the consequences of the successful siege of Louisburg. But we will not sadden ourselves with these doleful thoughts, when we are to witness the triumphal entry of the victors into the surrendered town.

The thundering of drums, irregularly beaten, grows more and more distinct, and the shattered strength of the western wall of Louisburg stretches out before the eye, forty feet in height, and far overtopped by a rock built citadel. In yonder breach the broken timber, fractured stones, and crumbling earth prove the effect of the provincial cannon. The drawbridge is down over the wide moat; the gate is open; and the general and British commodore are received by the French authorities beneath the dark and lofty portal arch. Through the massive gloom of this deep avenue there is a vista of the main street, bordered by high peaked houses, in the fashion of old France; the view is terminated by the centre square of the city, in the midst of which rises a stone cross; and shaven monks, and women with their children, are kneeling at its foot. A confused sobbing and half-stifled shrieks are heard, as the tumultuous advance of the conquering army becomes audible to those within the walls. By the light which falls through the archway, we perceive that a few months have somewhat changed the general's mien, giving it the freedom of one acquainted with peril, and accustomed to command; nor, amid hopes of more solid reward, does he appear insensible to the thought that posterity will remember his name among those renowned in arms. Sir Peter Warren, who receives with him the enemy's submission, is a rough and haughty English seaman, greedy of fame, but despising those who have won it for him. Pressing forward to the portal, sword in hand, comes a comical figure in a brown suit, and blue yarn stockings, with a huge frill sticking forth from his bosom, to which the whole man seems an appendage this is that famous worthy of Plymouth County, who went to the war with two plain shirts and a ruffled one, and is now about to solicit the post of governor in Louisburg. In close vicinity stands Vaughan, worn down with toil and exposure, the effect of which has fallen upon him at once in the moment of accomplished hope. The group is filled up by several British officers, who fold their arms, and look with scornful merriment at the provincial army, as it stretches far behind in garments of every hue, resembling an immense strip of patchwork carpeting thrown down over the uneven ground. In the nearer ranks we may discern the variety of ingredients that compose the mass. Here advance a row of stern, unmitigable-fanatics, each of whom clinches his teeth, and grasps his weapon with a fist of iron, at sight of the temples of the ancient faith, with the sunlight glittering on their cross-crowned spires. Others examine the surrounding country, and send scrutinizing glances through the gateway, anxious to select a spot, whither the good woman and her little ones in the Bay Province may be advantageously transported. Some, who drag their diseased limbs forward in weariness and pain, have made the wretched exchange of health or life for what share of fleeting glory may fall to them among four thousand men. But these are all exceptions, and the exulting feelings of the general host combine in an expression like that of a broad laugh on an honest countenance. They roll onward riotously, flourishing their muskets above their heads, shuffling their heavy heels into an instinctive dance, and roaring out some holy verse from the New England Psalmody, or those harsh old warlike stanzas which tell the story of "Lovell's Fight." Thus they pour along, till the battered town and the rabble of its conquerors, and the shouts, the drums, the singing, and the laughter, grow dim, and die away from Fancy's eye and ear.

The arms of Great Britain were not crowned by a more brilliant achievement during that unprosperous war; and, in adjusting the terms of a subsequent peace, Louisburg was an equivalent for many losses nearer home. The English, with very pardonable vanity, attributed the conquest chiefly to the valor of the naval force. On the continent of Europe, our fathers met with greater justice, and Voltaire has ranked this enterprise of the husbandmen of New England among the most remarkable events in the reign of Louis XV. The ostensible leaders did not fail of reward. Shirley, originally a lawyer, was commissioned in the regular army, and rose to the supreme military command in America. Warren, also, received honors and professional rank, and arrogated to himself, without scruple, the whole crop of laurels gathered at Louisburg. Pepperell was placed at the head of a royal regiment, and, first of his countrymen, was distinguished by the title of baronet. Vaughan alone, who had been soul of the deed from its adventurous conception till the triumphant close, and in every danger and every hardship had exhibited a rare union of ardor and perseverance,--Vaughan was entirely neglected, and died in London, whither he had gone to make known his claims. After the great era of his life, Sir William Pepperell did not distinguish himself either as a warrior or a statesman. He spent the remainder of his days in all the pomp of a colonial grandee, and laid down his aristocratic head among the humbler ashes of his fathers, just before the commencement of the earliest troubles between England and America.

THOMAS GREEN FESSENDEN.

Thomas Green Fessenden was the eldest of nine children of the Rev. Thomas Fessenden. He was born on the 22d of April, 1771, at Walpole, in New Hampshire, where his father, a man of learning and talent, was long settled in the ministry. On the maternal side, likewise, he was of clerical extraction; his mother, whose piety and amiable qualities are remembered by her descendants, being the daughter of the Rev. Samuel Kendal of New Salem. The early education of Thomas Green was chiefly at the common school of his native place, under the tuition of students from the college at Hanover; and such was his progress, that he became himself the instructor of a school in New Salem at the age of sixteen. He spent most of his youthful days, however, in bodily labor upon the farm, thus contributing to the support of a numerous family; and the practical knowledge of agriculture which he then obtained was long afterwards applied to the service of the public. Opportunities for cultivating his mind were afforded him, not only in his father's library, but by the more miscellaneous contents of a large bookstore. He had passed the age of twenty-one when his inclination for mental pursuits determined him to become a student at Dartmouth College. His father being able to give but little assistance, his chief resources at, college consisted in his wages as teacher of a village school during the vacations. At times, also, he gave instruction to an evening class in psalmody.

From his childhood upward, Mr. Fessenden had shown symptoms of that humorous turn which afterwards so strongly marked his writings; but his first effort in verse, as he himself told me, was made during his residence at college. The themes, or exercises, of his fellow students in English composition, whether prose or rhyme, were well characterized by the lack of native thought and feeling, the cold pedantry, the mimicry of classic models, common to all such productions. Mr. Fessenden had the good taste to disapprove of these vapid and spiritless performances, and resolved to strike out a new course for himself. On one occasion, when his classmates had gone through with their customary round of verbiage and threadbare sentiment, he electrified them and their instructor, President Wheelock, by reading "***Jonathan's Courtship***." There has never, to this day, been produced by any of our countrymen a more original and truly Yankee effusion. He had caught the rare art of sketching familiar manners, and of throwing into verse the very spirit of society as it existed around him; and he had imbued each line with a peculiar yet perfectly natural and homely humor. This excellent ballad compels me to regret, that, instead of becoming a satirist in politics and science, and wasting his strength on temporary and evanescent topics, he had not continued to be a rural poet. A volume of such sketches as "Jonathan's Courtship," describing various aspects of life among the yeomanry of New England, could not have failed to gain a permanent place in American literature. The effort in question met with unexampled success: it ran through the newspapers of the day, reappeared on the other side of the Atlantic, and was warmly applauded by the English critics; nor has it yet lost its popularity. New editions may be found every year at the ballad-stalls; and I saw last summer, on the veteran author's table, a broadside copy of his maiden poem, which he had himself bought in the street.

Mr. Fessenden passed through college with a fair reputation for scholarship, and took his degree in 1796. It had been his father's wish that he should imitate the example of sonic of his ancestors on both sides, by devoting himself to the ministry. He, however, preferred the law, and commenced the study of that profession at Rutland, in Vermont, with Nathaniel Chipman, then the most eminent practitioner in the State. After his admission to the bar, Mr. Chipman received him into partnership. But Mr. Fessenden was ill qualified to succeed in the profession of law, by his simplicity of character, and his utter inability to acquire an ordinary share of shrewdness and worldly wisdom. Moreover, the success of "***Jonathan's Courtship***," and other poetical effusions, had turned his thoughts from law to literature, and had procured him the acquaintance of several literary luminaries of those days; none of whose names, probably, have survived to our own generation, save that of Joseph Dennie, once esteemed the finest writer in America. His intercourse with these people tempted Mr. Fessenden to spend much time in writing for newspapers and periodicals. A taste for scientific pursuits still further diverted him from his legal studies, and soon engaged him in an affair which influenced the complexion of all his after-life.

A Mr. Langdon had brought forward a newly invented hydraulic machine, which was supposed to possess the power of raising water to a greater height than had hitherto been considered possible. A company of mechanics and others became interested in this machine, and appointed Mr. Fessenden their agent for the purpose of obtaining a patent in London. He was, likewise, a member of the company. Mr. Fessenden was urged to hasten his departure, in consequence of a report that certain persons had acquired the secret of the invention, and were determined to anticipate the proprietors in securing a patent. Scarcely time was allowed for testing the efficacy of the machine by a few hasty experiments, which, however, appeared satisfactory. Taking passage immediately, Mr. Fessenden arrived in London on the 4th of July, 1801, and waited on Mr. King, then our minister, by whom he was introduced to Mr. Nicholson, a gentleman of eminent scientific reputation. After thoroughly examining the invention, Mr. Nicholson gave an opinion unfavorable to its merits; and the question was soon settled by a letter from one of the Vermont proprietors to Mr. Fessenden, informing him that the apparent advantages of the machine had been found altogether deceptive. In short, Mr. Fessenden had been lured from his profession and country by as empty a bubble as that of the perpetual motion. Yet it is creditable both to his ability and energy, that, laying hold of what was really valuable in Langdon's contrivance; he constructed the model of a machine for raising water from coal-mines, and other great depths, by means of what he termed the "renovated pressure of the atmosphere." On communicating this invention to Mr. Nicholson and other eminent mechanicians, they acknowledged its originality and ingenuity, and thought that, in some situations, it might be useful. But the expenses of a patent in England, the difficulty of obtaining patronage for such a project, and the uncertainty of the result, were obstacles too weighty to be overcome. Mr. Fessenden threw aside the scheme, and, after a two months' residence in London, was preparing to return home, when a new and characteristic adventure arrested him.

He received a visit, at his lodging in the Strand, from a person whom he had never before seen, but who introduced himself to his good-will as being likewise an

American. His business was of a nature well calculated to excite Mr. Fessenden's interest. He produced the model of an ingenious contrivance for grinding corn. A patent had already been obtained; and a company, with the lord-mayor of London at its head, was associated for the construction of mills upon this new principle. The inventor, according to his own story, had disposed of one-fourth part of his patent for five hundred pounds, and was willing to accommodate his countryman with another fourth. After some inquiry into the stranger's character and the accuracy of his statements, Mr. Fessenden became a purchaser of the share that was offered him; on what terms is not stated, but probably such as to involve his whole property in the adventure. The result was disastrous. The lord-mayor soon withdrew his countenance from the project. It ultimately appeared that Mr. Fessenden was the only real purchaser of any part of the patent; and, as the original patentee shortly afterwards quitted the concern, the former was left to manage the business as he best could. With a perseverance not less characteristic than his credulity, he associated himself with four partners, and undertook to superintend the construction of one of these patent-mills upon the Thanes. But his associates, who were men of no respectability, thwarted his plans; and after much toil of body, as well as distress of mind, he found himself utterly ruined, friendless and penniless, in the midst of London. No other event could have been anticipated, when a man so devoid of guile was thrown among a set of crafty adventurers.

 Being now in the situation in which many a literary man before him had been, he remembered the success of his fugitive poems, and betook himself to the pen as his most natural resource. A subject was offered him, in which no other poet would have found a theme for the Muse. It seemed to be his fatality to form connections with schemers of all sorts; and he had become acquainted with Benjamin Douglas Perkins, the patentee of the famous metallic tractors. These implements were then in great vogue for the cure of inflammatory diseases, by removing the superfluous electricity. Perkinism, as the doctrine of metallic tractors was styled, had some converts among scientific men, and many among the people but was violently opposed by the regular corps of physicians and surgeons. Mr. Fessenden, as might be expected, was a believer in the efficacy of the tractors, and, at the request of Perkins, consented to make them the subject of a poem in Hudibrastic verse, the satire of which was to be levelled against their opponents. "Terrible Tractoration" was the result. It professes to be a poetical petition from Dr. Christopher Caustic, a medical gentleman who has been ruined by the success of the metallic tractors, and who applies to the Royal College of Physicians for relief and redress. The wits of the poor doctor have been somewhat shattered by his misfortunes; and, with crazy ingenuity, he contrives to heap ridicule on his medical brethren, under pretence of railing against Perkinism. The poem is in four cantos, the first of which is the best, and the most characteristic of the author. It is occupied with Dr. Caustic's description of his mechanical and scientific contrivances, embracing all sorts of possible and impossible projects; every one of which, however, has a ridiculous plausibility. The inexhaustible variety in which they flow forth proves the author's invention unrivalled in its way. It shows what had been the nature of Mr. Fessenden's mental toil during his residence in London, continually brooding over the miracles of mechanism and science, his enthusiasm for which had cost him so dear. Long afterwards, speaking of the first conception of this poem, the author told me that he had shaped it out during a solitary day's ramble in the outskirts of London; and the character of Dr. Caustic so strongly impressed itself on his mind, that, as he walked homeward through the crowded streets, he burst into frequent fits of laughter.

The truth is, that, in the sketch of this wild projector, Mr. Fessenden had caricatured some of his own features; and, when he laughed so heartily, it was at the perception of the resemblance.

"Terrible Tractoration" is a work of strange and grotesque ideas aptly expressed: its rhymes are of a most singular character, yet fitting each to each as accurately as echoes. As in all Mr. Fessenden's productions, there is great exactness in the language; the author's thoughts being thrown off as distinctly as impressions from a type. In regard to the pleasure to be derived from reading this poem, there is room for diversity of taste; but, that it is all original and remarkable work, no person competent to pass judgment on a literary question will deny. It was first published early in the year 1803, in an octavo pamphlet of above fifty pages. Being highly applauded by the principal reviews, and eagerly purchased by the public, a new edition appeared at the end of two months, in a volume of nearly two hundred pages, illustrated with engravings. It received the praise of Gifford, the severest of English critics. Its continued success encouraged the author to publish a volume of "Original Poems," consisting chiefly of his fugitive pieces from the American newspapers.

This, also, was favorably received. He was now, what so few of his countrymen have ever been, a popular author in London; and, in the midst of his triumphs, he bethought himself of his native land.

Mr. Fessenden returned to America in 1804. He came back poorer than he went, but with an honorable reputation, and with unstained integrity, although his evil fortune had connected him with men far unlike himself. His fame had preceded him across the Atlantic. Shortly before his arrival, an edition of "Terrible Tractoration" had been published at Philadelphia, with a prefatory memoir of the author, the tone of which proves that the American people felt themselves honored in the literary success of their countryman. Another edition appeared in New York, in 1806, considerably enlarged, with a new satire on the topics of the day. It is symptomatic of the course which the author had now adopted, that much of this new satire was directed against Democratic principles and the prominent upholders of them. This was soon followed by "Democracy Unveiled," a more elaborate attack on the same political party.

In "Democracy Unveiled," our friend Dr. Caustic appears as a citizen of the United States, and pours out six cantos of vituperative verse, with copious notes of the same tenor, on the heads of President Jefferson and his supporters. Much of the satire is unpardonably coarse. The literary merits of the work are inferior to those of "Terrible Tractoration "; but it is no less original and peculiar. Even where the matter is a mere versification of newspaper slander, Dr. Caustic's manner gives it an individuality not to be mistaken. The book passed through three editions in the course of a few months. Its most pungent portions were copied into all the opposition prints; its strange, jog- trot stanzas were familiar to every ear; and Mr. Fessenden may fairly be allowed the credit of having given expression to the feelings of the great Federal party.

On the 30th of August, 1806, Mr. Fessenden commenced the publication, at New York, of "*The Weekly Inspector*," a paper at first of eight, and afterwards of sixteen, octavo pages. It appeared every Saturday. The character of this journal was mainly political; but there are also a few flowers and sweet-scented twigs of literature intermixed among the nettles and burs, which alone flourish in the arena of party strife. Its columns are profusely enriched with scraps of satirical verse in which Dr. Caustic, in his capacity of ballad-maker to the Federal faction, spared not to celebrate every man or measure of government that was anywise susceptible of ridicule. Many of his prose articles are carefully and ably written, attacking not men so much as principles and measures; and his deeply felt anxiety for the welfare of his country sometimes gives an impressive dignity to his thoughts and style. The dread of French domination seems to have haunted him like a nightmare. But, in spite of the editor's satirical reputation, "*The Weekly Inspector*" was too conscientious a paper, too sparingly spiced with the red pepper of personal abuse, to succeed in those outrageous times. The publication continued but for a single year, at the end of which we find Mr. Fessenden's valedictory to his leaders. Its tone is despondent both as to the prospects of the country and his own private fortunes. The next token of his labors that has come under my notice is a small volume of verse, published at Philadelphia in 1809, and alliteratively entitled "Pills, Poetical, Political, and Philosophical; prescribed for the Purpose of purging the Public of Piddling Philosophers, Penny Poetasters, of Paltry Politicians, and Petty Partisans. By Peter Pepper-Box, Poet and Physician." This satire had been written during the embargo, but, not making its appearance till after the repeal of that measure, met with less success than "Democracy Unveiled."

Everybody who has known Mr. Fessenden must have wondered how the kindest hearted man in all the world could have likewise been the most noted satirist of his day. For my part, I have tried in vain to form a conception of my venerable and peaceful friend as a champion in the stormy strife of party, flinging mud full in the faces of his foes, and shouting forth the bitter laughter that rang from border to border of the land; and I can hardly believe, though well assured of it, that his antagonists should ever have meditated personal violence against the gentlest of human creatures. I am sure, at least, that Nature never meant him for a satirist. On careful examination of his works, I do not find in any of them the ferocity of the true bloodhound of literature, such as Swift, or Churchill, or Cobbett,--which fastens upon the throat of its victim, and would fain drink his lifeblood. In my opinion, Mr. Fessenden never felt the slightest personal ill-will against the objects of his satire, except, indeed, they had endeavored to detract from his literary reputation,--an offence which he resented with a poet's sensibility, and seldom failed to punish. With such exceptions, his works are not properly satirical, but the offspring of a mind inexhaustibly fertile in ludicrous ideas, which it appended to any topic in hand. At times, doubtless, the all-pervading frenzy of the times inspired him with a bitterness not his own. But, in the least defensible of his writings, he was influenced by an honest zeal for the public good. There was nothing mercenary in his connection with politics. To an antagonist who had taunted him with being poor, he calmly replied, that he "need not have been accused of the crime of poverty, could he have prostituted his principles to party purposes, and become the hireling assassin of the dominant faction." Nor can there be a doubt that the administration would gladly have purchased the pen of so popular a writer.

I have gained hardly any information of Mr. Fessenden's life between the years 1807 and 1812; at which latter period, and probably some time previous, he was settled at the village of Bellows Falls, on Connecticut River, in the practice of the law. In May of that year, he had the good fortune to become acquainted with Miss Lydia Tuttle, daughter of Mr. John Tuttle, an independent and intelligent farmer at Littleton, Mass. She was then on a visit in Vermont. After her return home, a correspondence ensued between this lady and Mr. Fessenden, and was continued till their marriage, in September, 1813. She was considerably younger than himself, but endowed with the qualities most desirable in the wife of such a man; and it would not be easy to overestimate how much his prosperity and happiness were increased by this union. Mrs. Fessenden could appreciate what was excellent in her husband, and supply what was deficient. In her affectionate good sense he found a substitute for the worldly sagacity which he did not possess, and could not learn. To her he intrusted the pecuniary cares, always so burdensome to a literary man. Her influence restrained him from such imprudent enterprises as had caused the misfortunes of his earlier years. She smoothed his path of life, and made it pleasant to him, and lengthened it; for, as he once told me (I believe it was while advising me to take, betimes, a similar treasure to myself), he would have been in his grave long ago, but for her care.

Mr. Fessenden continued to practise law at Bellows Falls till 1815, when he removed to Brattleborough, and assumed the editorship of "The Brattleborough Reporter," a political newspaper. The following year, in compliance with a pressing invitation from the inhabitants, he returned to Bellows Falls, and edited, with much success, a literary and political paper, called "*The Intelligencer*." He held this employment till the year 1822, at the same time practising law, and composing a volume of poetry, "*The Ladies' Monitor*," besides compiling several works in law, the arts, and agriculture. During this part of his life, he usually spent sixteen hours of the twenty-four in study. In 1822 he came to Boston as editor of "*The New England Farmer*," a weekly journal, the first established, and devoted principally to the diffusion of agricultural knowledge.

His management of the Farmer met unreserved approbation. Having been bred upon a farm, and passed much of his later life in the country, and being thoroughly conversant with the writers on rural economy, he was admirably qualified to conduct such a journal. It was extensively circulated throughout New England, and may be said to have fertilized the soil like rain from heaven. Numerous papers on the same plan sprung up in various parts of the country; but none attained the standard of their prototype. Besides his editorial labors, Mr. Fessenden published, from time to time, various compilations on agricultural subjects, or adaptations of English treatises to the use of the American husbandman. Verse he no longer wrote, except, now and then, an ode or song for some agricultural festivity. His poems, being connected with topics of temporary interest, ceased to be read, now that the metallic tractors were thrown aside, and that the blending and merging of parties had created an entire change of political aspects, since the days of "Democracy Unveiled." The poetic laurel withered among his gray hairs, and dropped away, leaf by leaf. His name, once the most familiar, was forgotten in the list of American bards. I know not that this oblivion was to be regretted. Mr. Fessenden, if my observation of his temperament be correct, was peculiarly sensitive and nervous in regard to the trials of authorship: a little censure did him more harm than much praise could do him good; and methinks the repose of total neglect was better for him than a feverish notoriety. Were it worth while to imagine any other course for the latter part of his life, which he made so useful and so honorable, it might be wished that he could have devoted himself entirely to scientific research. He had a strong taste for studies of that kind, and sometimes used to lament that his daily drudgery afforded him no leisure to compose a work on caloric, which subject he had thoroughly investigated.

In January, 1836, I became, and continued for a few months, an inmate of Mr. Fessenden's family. It was my first acquaintance with him. His image is before my mind's eye at this moment; slowly approaching me with a lamp in his hand, his hair gray, his face solemn and pale, his tall and portly figure bent with heavier infirmity than befitted his years. His dress, though he had improved in this particular since middle life, was marked by a truly scholastic negligence. He greeted me kindly, and with plain, old-fashioned courtesy; though I fancied that he somewhat regretted the interruption of his evening studies. After a few moments' talk, he invited me to accompany him to his study, and give my opinion on some passages of satirical verse, which were to be inserted in a new edition of "Terrible Tractoration." Years before, I had lighted on an illustrated copy of this poem, bestrewn with venerable dust, in a corner of a college library; and it seemed strange and whimsical that I should find it still in progress of composition, and be consulted about it by Dr. Caustic himself. While Mr. Fessenden read, I had leisure to glance around at his study, which was very characteristic of the man and his occupations. The table, and great part of the floor, were covered with books and pamphlets on agricultural subjects, newspapers from all quarters, manuscript articles for "*The New England Farmer*," and manuscript stanzas for "Terrible Tractoration." There was such a litter as always gathers around a literary man. It bespoke, at once, Mr. Fessenden's amiable temper and his abstracted habits, that several members of the family, old and young, were sitting in the room, and engaged in conversation, apparently without giving him the least disturbance. A specimen of Dr. Caustic's inventive genius was seen in the "Patent Steam and Hot-Water Stove," which heated the apartment, and kept up a pleasant singing sound, like that of a teakettle, thereby making the fireside more cheerful. It appears to me, that, having no children of flesh and blood, Mr. Fessenden had contracted a fatherly fondness for this stove, as being his mental progeny; and it must be owned that the stove well deserved his affection, and repaid it with much warmth.

The new edition of "Tractoration" came out not long afterwards. It was noticed with great kindness by the press, but was not warmly received by the public. Mr. Fessenden imputed the failure, in part, to the illiberality of the "trade," and avenged himself by a little poem, in his best style, entitled "Wooden Booksellers"; so that the last blow of his satirical scourge was given in the good old cause of authors against publishers.

Notwithstanding a wide difference of age, and many more points of dissimilarity than of resemblance, Mr. Fessenden and myself soon became friends. His partiality seemed not to be the result of any nice discrimination of my good and evil qualities (for he had no acuteness in that way), but to be given instinctively, like the affection of a child. On my part, I loved the old man because his heart was as transparent as a fountain; and I could see nothing in it but integrity and purity, and simple faith in his fellow-men, and good-will towards all the world. His character was so open, that I did not need to correct my original conception of it. He never seemed to me like a new acquaintance, but as one with whom I had been familiar from my infancy. Yet he was a rare man, such as few meet with in the course of a lifetime. It is remarkable, that, with such kindly affections, Mr. Fessenden was so deeply absorbed in thought and study as scarcely to allow himself time for domestic and social enjoyment. During the winter when I first knew him, his mental drudgery was almost continual. Besides "*The New England Farmer*," lie had the editorial charge of two other journals,-- "*The Horticultural Register*," and "*The Silk Manual*"; in addition to which employment, he was a member of the State legislature, and took some share in the debates. The new matter of "Terrible Tractoration" likewise cost him intense thought. Sometimes I used to meet him in the street, making his way onward apparently by a sort of instinct; while his eyes took note of nothing, and would, perhaps, pass over my face without sign of recognition. He confessed to me that he was apt to go astray when intent on rhyme. With so much to abstract him from outward life, he could hardly be said to live in the world that was bustling around him. Almost the only relaxation that he allowed himself was an occasional performance on a bass-viol which stood in the corner of his study, and from which he loved to elicit some old-fashioned tune of soothing potency. At meal-times, however, dragged down and harassed as his spirits were, he brightened up, and generally gladdened the whole table with a flash of Dr. Caustic's honor.

Had I anticipated being Mr. Fessenden's biographer, I might have drawn from him many details that would have been well worth remembering. But he had not the tendency of most men in advanced life, to be copious in personal reminiscences; nor did he often speak of the noted writers and politicians with whom the chances of earlier years had associated him. Indeed, lacking a turn for observation of character, his former companions had passed before him like images in a mirror, giving him little knowledge of their inner nature. Moreover, till his latest day, he was more inclined to form prospects for the future than to dwell upon the past. I remember the last time, save one, that we ever met--I found him on the bed, suffering with a dizziness of the brain. He roused himself, however, and grew very cheerful; talking, with a youthful glow of fancy, about emigrating to Illinois, where he possessed a farm, and picturing a new life for both of us in that Western region. It has since come to my memory, that, while he spoke, there was a purple flush across his brow,--the harbinger of death.

I saw him but once more alive. On the thirteenth day of November last, while on my way to Boston, expecting shortly to take him by the hand, a letter met me with an invitation to his funeral--he had been struck with apoplexy on Friday evening, three days before, and had lain insensible till Saturday night, when he expired. The burial took place at Mount Auburn on the ensuing Tuesday. It was a gloomy day; for the first snowstorm of the season had been drifting through the air since morning; and the "Garden of Graves" looked the dreariest spot on earth. The snow came down so fast, that it covered the coffin in its passage from the hearse to the sepulchre. The few male friends who had followed to the cemetery descended into the tomb; and it was there that I took my last glance at the features of a man who will hold a place in my remembrance apart from other men. He was like no other. In his long pathway through life, from his cradle to the place where we had now laid him, he had come, a man indeed in intellect and achievement, but, in guileless simplicity, a child. Dark would have been the hour, if, when we closed the door of the tomb upon his perishing mortality, we had believed that our friend was there.

It is contemplated to erect a monument, by subscription, to Mr. Fessenden's memory. It is right that he should be thus honored. Mount Auburn will long remain a desert, barren of consecrated marbles, if worth like his be yielded to oblivion. Let his grave be marked out, that the yeomen of New England may know where he sleeps; for he was their familiar friend, and has visited them at all their firesides. He has toiled for them at seed-time and harvest: he has scattered the good grain in every field; and they have garnered the increase. Mark out his grave as that of one worthy to be remembered both in the literary and political annals of our country, and let the laurel be carved on his memorial stone; for it will cover the ashes of a man of genius.

JONATHAN CILLEY.

The subject of this brief memorial had barely begun to be an actor in the great scenes where his part could not have failed to be a prominent one. The nation did not have time to recognize him. His death, aside from the shock with which the manner of it has thrilled every bosom, is looked upon merely as causing a vacancy in the delegation of his State, which a new member may fill as creditably as the departed. It will, perhaps, be deemed praise enough to say of Cilley, that he would have proved himself an active and efficient partisan. But those who knew him longest and most intimately, conscious of his high talents and rare qualities, his energy of mind and force of character, must claim much more than such a meed for their lost friend. They feel that not merely a party nor a section, but our collective country, has lost a man who had the heart and the ability to serve her well. It would be doing injustice to the hopes which lie withered upon his untimely grave, if, in paying a farewell tribute to his memory, we were to ask a narrower sympathy than that of the people at large. May no bitterness of party prejudices influence him who writes, nor those, of whatever political opinions, who may read!

Jonathan Cilley was born at Nottingham, N. H., on the 2d of July, 1802. His grandfather, Colonel Joseph Cilley, commanded a New Hampshire regiment during the Revolutionary War, and established a character for energy and intrepidity, of which more than one of his descendants have proved themselves the inheritors. Greenleaf Cilley, son of the preceding, died in 1808, leaving a family of four sons and three daughters. The aged mother of this family, and the three daughters, are still living. Of the sons, the only survivor is Joseph Cilley, who was an officer in the late war, and served with great distinction on the Canadian frontier. Jonathan, being desirous of a liberal education, commenced his studies at Atkinson Academy, at about the age of seventeen, and became a member of the freshman class of Bowdoin College, Brunswick, Me., in 1821. Inheriting but little property from his father, he adopted the usual expedient of a young New-Englander in similar circumstances, and gained a small income by teaching a country school during the winter months both before and, after his entrance at college.

Cilley's character and standing at college afforded high promise of usefulness and distinction in after-life. Though not the foremost scholar of his class, he stood in the front rank, and probably derived all the real benefit from the prescribed course of study that it could bestow on so practical a mind. His true education consisted in the exercise of those faculties which fitted him to be a popular leader. His influence among his fellow-students was probably greater than that of any other individual; and he had already made himself powerful in that limited sphere, by a free and natural eloquence, a flow of pertinent ideas in language of unstudied appropriateness, which seemed always to accomplish precisely the result on which he had calculated. This gift was sometimes displayed in class meetings, when measures important to those concerned were under discussion; sometimes in mock trials at law, when judge, jury, lawyers, prisoner, and witnesses were personated by the students, and Cilley played the part of a fervid and successful advocate; and, besides these exhibitions of power, he regularly trained himself in the forensic debates of a literary society, of which he afterwards became president. Nothing could be less artificial than his style of oratory. After filling his mind with the necessary information, he trusted everything else to his mental warmth and the inspiration of the moment, and poured himself out with an earnest and irresistible simplicity. There was a singular contrast between the flow of thought from his lips, and the coldness and restraint with which he wrote; and though, in maturer life, he acquired a considerable facility in exercising the pen, he always felt the tongue to be his peculiar instrument.

In private intercourse, Cilley possessed a remarkable fascination. It was impossible not to regard him with the kindliest feelings, because his companions were intuitively certain of a like kindliness on his part. He had a power of sympathy which enabled him to understand every character, and hold communion with human nature in all its varieties. He never shrank from the intercourse of man with man; and it was to his freedom in this particular that he owed much of his subsequent popularity among a people who are accustomed to take a personal interest in the men whom they elevate to office. In few words, let us characterize him at the outset of life as a young man of quick and powerful intellect, endowed with sagacity and tact, yet frank and free in his mode of action, ambitious of good influence, earnest, active, and persevering, with an elasticity and cheerful strength of mind which made difficulties easy, and the struggle with them a pleasure. Mingled with the amiable qualities that were like sunshine to his friends, there were harsher and sterner traits, which fitted him to make head against an adverse world; but it was only at the moment of need that the iron framework of his character became perceptible.

Immediately on quitting college, Mr. Cilley took up his residence in Thomaston, and began the study of law in the office of John Ruggles, Esq., now a senator in Congress. Mr. Ruggles being then a prominent member of the Democratic party, it was natural that the pupil should lend his aid to promote the political views of his instructor, especially as he would thus uphold the principles which he had cherished from boyhood. From year to year, the election of Mr. Ruggles to the State legislature was strongly opposed. Cilley's services in overcoming this opposition were too valuable to be dispensed with; and thus, at a period when most young men still stand aloof from the world, he had already taken his post as a leading politician. He afterwards found cause to regret that so much time had been abstracted from his professional studies; nor did the absorbing and exciting nature of his political career afford him any subsequent opportunity to supply the defects of his legal education. He was admitted an attorney-at-law in 1829, and in April of the same year was married to Miss Deborah Prince, daughter of Hon. Hezekiah Prince of Thomaston, where Mr. Cilley continued to reside, and entered upon the practice of his profession.

In 1831, Mr. Ruggles having been appointed a judge of the court of common pleas, it became necessary to send a new representative from Thomaston to the legislature of the State. Mr. Cilley was brought forward as the Democratic candidate, obtained his election, and took his seat in January, 1832. But in the course of this year the friendly relations between Judge Ruggles and Mr. Cilley were broken off. Time former gentleman, it appears, had imbibed the idea that his political aspirations (which were then directed towards a seat in the Senate of the United States) did not receive all the aid which he was disposed to claim from the influence of his late pupil. When, therefore, Mr. Cilley was held up as a candidate for re-election to the legislature, the whole strength of Judge Ruggles and his adherents was exerted against him. This was the first act and declaration of a political hostility, which was too warm and earnest not to become, in some degree, personal, and which rendered Mr. Cilley's subsequent career a continual struggle with those to whom he might naturally have looked for friendship and support. It sets his abilities and force of character in the strongest light, to view him, at the very outset of public life, without the aid of powerful connections, an isolated young man, forced into a position of hostility, not merely with the enemies of his party, but likewise with a large body of its adherents, even accused of treachery to its principles, yet gaining triumph after triumph, and making his way steadily onward. Surely his was a mental and moral energy which death alone could have laid prostrate.

We have the testimony of those who knew Mr. Cilley well, that his own feelings were never so embittered by those conflicts as to prevent him from interchanging the courtesies of society with his most violent opponents. While their resentments rendered his very presence intolerable to them, he could address them with as much ease and composure as if their mutual relations had been those of perfect harmony. There was no affectation in this: it was the good-natured consciousness of his own strength that enabled him to keep his temper: it was the same chivalrous sentiment which impels hostile warriors to shake hands in the intervals of battle. Mr. Cilley was slow to withdraw his confidence from any man whom he deemed a friend; and it has been mentioned as almost his only weak point, that he was too apt to suffer himself to be betrayed before he would condescend to suspect. His prejudices, however, when once adopted, partook of the depth and strength of his character, and could not be readily overcome. He loved to subdue his foes; but no man could use a triumph more generously than he.

Let us resume our narrative. In spite of the opposition of Judge Ruggles and his friends, combined with that of the Whigs, Mr. Cilley was re-elected to the legislature of 1833, and was equally successful in each of the succeeding years, until his election to Congress. He was five successive years the representative of Thomaston. In 1834, when Mr. Dunlap was nominated as the Democratic candidate for governor, Mr. Cilley gave his support to Governor Smith, in the belief that the substitution of a new candidate had been unfairly effected. He considered it a stratagem intended to promote the election of Judge Ruggles to the Senate of the United States. Early in the legislative session of the same year, the Ruggles party obtained a temporary triumph over Mr. Cilley, effected his expulsion from the Democratic caucuses, and attempted to stigmatize him as a traitor to his political friends. But Mr. Cilley's high and honorable course was erelong understood and appreciated by his party and the people. He told them, openly and boldly, that they might undertake to expel him from their caucuses; but they could not expel him from the Democratic party: they might stigmatize him with any appellation they might choose; but they could not reach the height on which he stood, nor shake his position with the people. But a few weeks had elapsed, and Mr. Cilley was the acknowledged head and leader of that party in the legislature. During the same session, Mr. Speaker Clifford (one of the friends of Judge Ruggles) being appointed attorney-general, the Ruggles party were desirous of securing the election of another of their adherents to the chair; but, as it was obvious that Mr. Cilley's popularity would gain him the place, the incumbent was induced to delay his resignation till the end of the term. At the session of 1835, Messrs. Cilley, Davee, and McCrote being candidates for the chair, Mr. Cilley withdrew in favor of Mr. Davee. That gentleman was accordingly elected; but, being soon afterwards appointed sheriff of Somerset County, Mr. Cilley succeeded him as speaker, and filled the same office during the session of 1836. All parties awarded him the praise of being the best presiding officer that the house ever had.

In 1836, he was nominated by a large portion of the Democratic electors of the Lincoln Congressional District as their candidate for Congress. That district has recently shown itself to possess a decided Whig majority; and this would have been equally the case in 1836, had any other man than Mr. Cilley appeared on the Democratic side. He had likewise to contend, as in all the former scenes of his political life, with that portion of his own party which adhered to Mr. Ruggles. There was still another formidable obstacle, in the high character of Judge Bailey, who then represented the district, and was a candidate for re-election. All these difficulties, however, served only to protract the contest, but could not snatch the victory from Mr. Cilley, who obtained a majority of votes at the third trial. It was a fatal triumph.

In the summer of 1837, a few months after his election to Congress, I met Mr.

Cilley for the first time since early youth, when he had been to me almost as an elder brother. The two or three days which I spent in his neighborhood enabled us to renew our former intimacy. In his person there was very little change, and that little was for the better. He had an impending brow, deep-set eyes, and a thin and thoughtful countenance, which, in his abstracted moments, seemed almost stern; but, in the intercourse of society, it was brightened with a kindly smile, that will live in the recollection of all who knew him. His manners had not a fastidious polish, but were characterized by the simplicity of one who had dwelt remote from cities, holding free companionship with the yeomen of the land. I thought him as true a representative of the people as ever theory could portray. His earlier and later habits of life, his feelings, partialities, and prejudices, were those of the people: the strong and shrewd sense which constituted so marked a feature of his mind was but a higher degree of the popular intellect. He loved the people and respected them, and was prouder of nothing than of his brotherhood with those who had intrusted their public interests to his care. His continual struggles in the political arena had strengthened his bones and sinews: opposition had kept him ardent; while success had cherished the generous warmth of his nature, and assisted the growth both of his powers and sympathies. Disappointment might have soured and contracted him; but it appeared to me that his triumphant warfare had been no less beneficial to his heart than to his mind. I was aware, indeed, that his harsher traits had grown apace with his milder ones; that he possessed iron resolution, indomitable perseverance, and an almost terrible energy; but these features had imparted no hardness to his character in private intercourse. In the hour of public need, these strong qualities would have shown themselves the most prominent ones, and would have encouraged his countrymen to rally round him as one of their natural leaders.

In his private and domestic relations, Mr. Cilley was most exemplary; and he enjoyed no less happiness than he conferred. He had been the father of four children, two of whom were in the grave, leaving, I thought, a more abiding impression of tenderness and regret than the death of infants usually makes on the masculine mind. Two boys--the elder, seven or eight years of age; and the younger, two--still remained to him; and the fondness of these children for their father, their evident enjoyment of his society, was proof enough of his gentle and amiable character within the precincts of his family. In that bereaved household, there is now another child, whom the father never saw. Mr. Cilley's domestic habits were simple and primitive to a degree unusual, in most parts of our country, among men of so eminent a station as he had attained. It made me smile, though with anything but scorn, in contrast to the aristocratic stateliness which I have witnessed elsewhere, to see him driving home his own cow after a long search for her through the village. That trait alone would have marked him as a man whose greatness lay within himself. He appeared to take much interest in the cultivation of his garden, and was very fond of flowers. He kept bees, and told me that he loved to sit for whole hours by the hives, watching the labors of the insects, and soothed by the hum with which they filled the air. I glance at these minute particulars of his daily life, because they form so strange a contrast with the circumstances of his death. Who could have believed, that, with his thoroughly New England character, in so short a time after I had seen him in that peaceful and happy home, among those simple occupations and pure enjoyments, he would be stretched in his own blood, slain for an almost impalpable punctilio!

It is not my purpose to dwell upon Mr. Cilley's brief career in Congress. Brief as it was, his character and talents had more than begun to be felt, and would soon have linked his name with the history of every important measure, and have borne it onward with the progress of the principles which he supported. He was not eager to seize opportunities of thrusting himself into notice; but, when time and the occasion summoned him, he came forward, and poured forth his ready and natural eloquence with as much effect in the councils of the nation as he had done in those of his own State. With every effort that he made, the hopes of his party rested more decidedly upon him, as one who would hereafter be found in the vanguard of many a Democratic victory. Let me spare myself the details of the awful catastrophe by which all those proud hopes perished; for I write with a blunted pen and a head benumbed, and am the less able to express my feelings as they lie deep at heart, and inexhaustible.

On the 23d of February last, Mr. Cilley received a challenge from Mr. Graves of Kentucky, through the hands of Mr. Wise of Virginia. This measure, as is declared in the challenge itself, was grounded on Mr. Cilley's refusal to receive a message, of which Mr. Graves had been the bearer, from a person of disputed respectability; although no exception to that person's character had been expressed by Mr. Cilley;

nor need such inference have been drawn, unless Mr. Graves were conscious that public opinion held his friend in a doubtful light. The challenge was accepted, and the parties met on the following day. They exchanged two shots with rifles. After each shot, a conference was held between the friends of both parties, and the most generous avowals of respect and kindly feeling were made on the part of Cilley towards his antagonist, but without avail. A third shot was exchanged; and Mr. Cilley fell dead into the arms of one of his friends. While I write, a Committee of Investigation is sitting upon this affair: but the public has not waited for its award; and the writer, in accordance with the public, has formed his opinion on the official statement of Messrs. Wise and Jones. A challenge was never given on a more shadowy pretext; a duel was never pressed to a fatal close in the face of such open kindness as was expressed by Mr. Cilley: and the conclusion is inevitable, that Mr. Graves and his principal second, Mr. Wise, have gone further than their own dreadful code will warrant them, and overstepped the imaginary distinction, which, on their own principles, separates manslaughter from murder.

Alas that over the grave of a dear friend, my sorrow for the bereavement must be mingled with another grief,--that he threw away such a life in so miserable a cause! Why, as he was true to the Northern character in all things else, did be swerve from his Northern principles in this final scene? But his error was a generous one, since he fought for what he deemed the honor of New England; and, now that death has paid the forfeit, the most rigid may forgive him. If that dark pitfall--that bloody grave--had not lain in the midst of his path, whither, whither might it not have led him! It has ended there: yet so strong was my conception of his energies, so like destiny did it appear that he should achieve everything at which he aimed, that even now my fancy will not dwell upon his grave, but pictures him still amid the struggles and triumphs of the present and the future.

1838.

www.bookjungle.com *email: sales@bookjungle.com fax: 630-214-0564 mail: Book Jungle PO Box 2226 Champaign, IL 61825*

The Codes Of Hammurabi And Moses
W. W. Davies

QTY

The discovery of the Hammurabi Code is one of the greatest achievements of archaeology, and is of paramount interest, not only to the student of the Bible, but also to all those interested in ancient history...

Religion ISBN: *1-59462-338-4* Pages:132 *MSRP $12.95*

The Theory of Moral Sentiments
Adam Smith

QTY

This work from 1749. contains original theories of conscience amd moral judgment and it is the foundation for systemof morals.

Philosophy ISBN: *1-59462-777-0* Pages:536 *MSRP $19.95*

Jessica's First Prayer
Hesba Stretton

QTY

In a screened and secluded corner of one of the many railway-bridges which span the streets of London there could be seen a few years ago, from five o'clock every morning until half past eight, a tidily set-out coffee-stall, consisting of a trestle and board, upon which stood two large tin cans, with a small fire of charcoal burning under each so as to keep the coffee boiling during the early hours of the morning when the work-people were thronging into the city on their way to their daily toil...

Childrens ISBN: *1-59462-373-2* Pages:84 *MSRP $9.95*

My Life and Work
Henry Ford

QTY

Henry Ford revolutionized the world with his implementation of mass production for the Model T automobile. Gain valuable business insight into his life and work with his own auto-biography... "We have only started on our development of our country we have not as yet, with all our talk of wonderful progress, done more than scratch the surface. The progress has been wonderful enough but..."

Biographies/ ISBN: *1-59462-198-5* Pages:300 *MSRP $21.95*

www.bookjungle.com *email: sales@bookjungle.com fax: 630-214-0564 mail: Book Jungle PO Box 2226 Champaign, IL 61825*

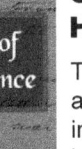

The Art of Cross-Examination
Francis Wellman

QTY

I presume it is the experience of every author, after his first book is published upon an important subject, to be almost overwhelmed with a wealth of ideas and illustrations which could readily have been included in his book, and which to his own mind, at least, seem to make a second edition inevitable. Such certainly was the case with me; and when the first edition had reached its sixth impression in five months, I rejoiced to learn that it seemed to my publishers that the book had met with a sufficiently favorable reception to justify a second and considerably enlarged edition. ..

Reference   ISBN: *1-59462-647-2*

Pages: 412
MSRP $19.95

On the Duty of Civil Disobedience
Henry David Thoreau

QTY

Thoreau wrote his famous essay, On the Duty of Civil Disobedience, as a protest against an unjust but popular war and the immoral but popular institution of slave-owning. He did more than write—he declined to pay his taxes, and was hauled off to gaol in consequence. Who can say how much this refusal of his hastened the end of the war and of slavery?

Law   ISBN: *1-59462-747-9*

Pages: 48
MSRP $7.45

Dream Psychology Psychoanalysis for Beginners
Sigmund Freud

QTY

Sigmund Freud, born Sigismund Schlomo Freud (May 6, 1856 - September 23, 1939), was a Jewish-Austrian neurologist and psychiatrist who co-founded the psychoanalytic school of psychology. Freud is best known for his theories of the unconscious mind, especially involving the mechanism of repression; his redefinition of sexual desire as mobile and directed towards a wide variety of objects; and his therapeutic techniques, especially his understanding of transference in the therapeutic relationship and the presumed value of dreams as sources of insight into unconscious desires.

Psychology   ISBN: *1-59462-905-6*

Pages: 196
MSRP $15.45

The Miracle of Right Thought
Orison Swett Marden

QTY

Believe with all of your heart that you will do what you were made to do. When the mind has once formed the habit of holding cheerful, happy, prosperous pictures, it will not be easy to form the opposite habit. It does not matter how improbable or how far away this realization may see, or how dark the prospects may be, if we visualize them as best we can, as vividly as possible, hold tenaciously to them and vigorously struggle to attain them, they will gradually become actualized, realized in the life. But a desire, a longing without endeavor, a yearning abandoned or held indifferently will vanish without realization.

Self Help   ISBN: *1-59462-644-8*

Pages: 360
MSRP $25.45

www.bookjungle.com email: sales@bookjungle.com fax: 630-214-0564 mail: Book Jungle PO Box 2226 Champaign, IL 61825

QTY

	Title	ISBN	Price
☐	**The Rosicrucian Cosmo-Conception Mystic Christianity** by *Max Heindel*	1-59462-188-8	$38.95
	The Rosicrucian Cosmo-conception is not dogmatic, neither does it appeal to any other authority than the reason of the student. It is: not controversial, but is: sent forth in the, hope that it may help to clear... *New Age/Religion Pages 646*		
☐	**Abandonment To Divine Providence** by *Jean-Pierre de Caussade*	1-59462-228-0	$25.95
	"The Rev. Jean Pierre de Caussade was one of the most remarkable spiritual writers of the Society of Jesus in France in the 18th Century. His death took place at Toulouse in 1751. His works have gone through many editions and have been republished... *Inspirational/Religion Pages 400*		
☐	**Mental Chemistry** by *Charles Haanel*	1-59462-192-6	$23.95
	Mental Chemistry allows the change of material conditions by combining and appropriately utilizing the power of the mind. Much like applied chemistry creates something new and unique out of careful combinations of chemicals the mastery of mental chemistry... *New Age Pages 354*		
☐	**The Letters of Robert Browning and Elizabeth Barret Barrett 1845-1846 vol II** by *Robert Browning and Elizabeth Barrett*	1-59462-193-4	$35.95
	Biographies Pages 596		
☐	**Gleanings In Genesis (volume I)** by *Arthur W. Pink*	1-59462-130-6	$27.45
	Appropriately has Genesis been termed "the seed plot of the Bible" for in it we have, in germ form, almost all of the great doctrines which are afterwards fully developed in the books of Scripture which follow... *Religion/Inspirational Pages 420*		
☐	**The Master Key** by *L. W. de Laurence*	1-59462-001-6	$30.95
	In no branch of human knowledge has there been a more lively increase of the spirit of research during the past few years than in the study of Psychology, Concentration and Mental Discipline. The requests for authentic lessons in Thought Control, Mental Discipline and... *New Age/Business Pages 422*		
☐	**The Lesser Key Of Solomon Goetia** by *L. W. de Laurence*	1-59462-092-X	$9.95
	This translation of the first book of the "Lemegton" which is now for the first time made accessible to students of Talismanic Magic was done, after careful collation and edition, from numerous Ancient Manuscripts in Hebrew, Latin, and French... *New Age/Occult Pages 92*		
☐	**Rubaiyat Of Omar Khayyam** by *Edward Fitzgerald*	1-59462-332-5	$13.95
	Edward Fitzgerald, whom the world has already learned, in spite of his own efforts to remain within the shadow of anonymity, to look upon as one of the rarest poets of the century, was born at Bredfield, in Suffolk, on the 31st of March, 1809. He was the third son of John Purcell... *Music Pages 172*		
☐	**Ancient Law** by *Henry Maine*	1-59462-128-4	$29.95
	The chief object of the following pages is to indicate some of the earliest ideas of mankind, as they are reflected in Ancient Law, and to point out the relation of those ideas to modern thought. *Religion/History Pages 452*		
☐	**Far-Away Stories** by *William J. Locke*	1-59462-129-2	$19.45
	"Good wine needs no bush, but a collection of mixed vintages does. And this book is just such a collection. Some of the stories I do not want to remain buried for ever in the museum files of dead magazine-numbers an author's not unpardonable vanity..." *Fiction Pages 272*		
☐	**Life of David Crockett** by *David Crockett*	1-59462-250-7	$27.45
	"Colonel David Crockett was one of the most remarkable men of the times in which he lived. Born in humble life, but gifted with a strong will, an indomitable courage, and unremitting perseverance... *Biographies/New Age Pages 424*		
☐	**Lip-Reading** by *Edward Nitchie*	1-59462-206-X	$25.95
	Edward B. Nitchie, founder of the New York School for the Hard of Hearing, now the Nitchie School of Lip-Reading, Inc, wrote "LIP-READING Principles and Practice". The development and perfecting of this meritorious work on lip-reading was an undertaking... *How-to Pages 400*		
☐	**A Handbook of Suggestive Therapeutics, Applied Hypnotism, Psychic Science** by *Henry Munro*	1-59462-214-0	$24.95
	Health/New Age/Health/Self-help Pages 376		
☐	**A Doll's House: and Two Other Plays** by *Henrik Ibsen*	1-59462-112-8	$19.95
	Henrik Ibsen created this classic when in revolutionary 1848 Rome. Introducing some striking concepts in playwriting for the realist genre, this play has been studied the world over. *Fiction/Classics/Plays 308*		
☐	**The Light of Asia** by *sir Edwin Arnold*	1-59462-204-3	$13.95
	In this poetic masterpiece, Edwin Arnold describes the life and teachings of Buddha. The man who was to become known as Buddha to the world was born as Prince Gautama of India but he rejected the worldly riches and abandoned the reigns of power when... *Religion/History/Biographies Pages 170*		
☐	**The Complete Works of Guy de Maupassant** by *Guy de Maupassant*	1-59462-157-8	$16.95
	"For days and days, nights and nights, I had dreamed of that first kiss which was to consecrate our engagement, and I knew not on what spot I should put my lips..." *Fiction/Classics Pages 240*		
☐	**The Art of Cross-Examination** by *Francis L. Wellman*	1-59462-309-0	$26.95
	Written by a renowned trial lawyer, Wellman imparts his experience and uses case studies to explain how to use psychology to extract desired information through questioning. *How-to/Science/Reference Pages 408*		
☐	**Answered or Unanswered?** by *Louisa Vaughan*	1-59462-248-5	$10.95
	Miracles of Faith in China *Religion Pages 112*		
☐	**The Edinburgh Lectures on Mental Science (1909)** by *Thomas*	1-59462-008-3	$11.95
	This book contains the substance of a course of lectures recently given by the writer in the Queen Street Hall, Edinburgh. Its purpose is to indicate the Natural Principles governing the relation between Mental Action and Material Conditions... *New Age/Psychology Pages 148*		
☐	**Ayesha** by *H. Rider Haggard*	1-59462-301-5	$24.95
	Verily and indeed it is the unexpected that happens! Probably if there was one person upon the earth from whom the Editor of this, and of a certain previous history, did not expect to hear again... *Classics Pages 380*		
☐	**Ayala's Angel** by *Anthony Trollope*	1-59462-352-X	$29.95
	The two girls were both pretty, but Lucy who was twenty-one who supposed to be simple and comparatively unattractive, whereas Ayala was credited, as her Bombwhat romantic name might show, with poetic charm and a taste for romance. Ayala when her father died was nineteen... *Fiction Pages 484*		
☐	**The American Commonwealth** by *James Bryce*	1-59462-286-8	$34.45
	An interpretation of American democratic political theory. It examines political mechanics and society from the perspective of Scotsman James Bryce *Politics Pages 572*		
☐	**Stories of the Pilgrims** by *Margaret P. Pumphrey*	1-59462-116-0	$17.95
	This book explores pilgrims religious oppression in England as well as their escape to Holland and eventual crossing to America on the Mayflower, and their early days in New England... *History Pages 268*		

www.bookjungle.com email: sales@bookjungle.com fax: 630-214-0564 mail: Book Jungle PO Box 2226 Champaign, IL 61825

Title	ISBN	Price	QTY
The Fasting Cure by *Sinclair Upton* — In the Cosmopolitan Magazine for May, 1910, and in the Contemporary Review (London) for April, 1910, I published an article dealing with my experiences in fasting. I have written a great many magazine articles, but never one which attracted so much attention... *New Age/Self Help/Health Pages 164*	*1-59462-222-1*	**$13.95**	☐
Hebrew Astrology by *Sepharial* — In these days of advanced thinking it is a matter of common observation that we have left many of the old landmarks behind and that we are now pressing forward to greater heights and to a wider horizon than that which represented the mind-content of our progenitors... *Astrology Pages 144*	*1-59462-308-2*	**$13.45**	☐
Thought Vibration or The Law of Attraction in the Thought World by *William Walker Atkinson* — *Psychology/Religion Pages 144*	*1-59462-127-6*	**$12.95**	☐
Optimism by *Helen Keller* — Helen Keller was blind, deaf, and mute since 19 months old, yet famously learned how to overcome these handicaps, communicate with the world, and spread her lectures promoting optimism. An inspiring read for everyone... *Biographies/Inspirational Pages 84*	*1-59462-108-X*	**$15.95**	☐
Sara Crewe by *Frances Burnett* — In the first place, Miss Minchin lived in London. Her home was a large, dull, tall one, in a large, dull square, where all the houses were alike, and all the sparrows were alike, and where all the door-knockers made the same heavy sound... *Childrens/Classic Pages 88*	*1-59462-360-0*	**$9.45**	☐
The Autobiography of Benjamin Franklin by *Benjamin Franklin* — The Autobiography of Benjamin Franklin has probably been more extensively read than any other American historical work, and no other book of its kind has had such ups and downs of fortune. Franklin lived for many years in England, where he was agent... *Biographies/History Pages 332*	*1-59462-135-7*	**$24.95**	☐

Name	
Email	
Telephone	
Address	
City, State ZIP	

☐ Credit Card   ☐ Check / Money Order

Credit Card Number	
Expiration Date	
Signature	

Please Mail to: Book Jungle
PO Box 2226
Champaign, IL 61825
or Fax to: 630-214-0564

ORDERING INFORMATION
web: www.bookjungle.com
email: sales@bookjungle.com
fax: 630-214-0564
mail: Book Jungle PO Box 2226 Champaign, IL 61825
or PayPal to sales@bookjungle.com

Please contact us for bulk discounts

DIRECT-ORDER TERMS

20% Discount if You Order Two or More Books
Free Domestic Shipping!
Accepted: Master Card, Visa, Discover, American Express

www.ingramcontent.com/pod-product-compliance
Lightning Source LLC
Chambersburg PA
CBHW081330040426
42453CB00013B/2367